For Every Field

For Every Field

Of Hope and Promise

AUDREY McHUGH

RESOURCE *Publications* • Eugene, Oregon

FOR EVERY FIELD
Of Hope and Promise

Resource Publications
An Imprint of Wipf and Stock Publishers
199 W. 8th Ave., Suite 3
Eugene, OR 97401

www.wipfandstock.com

PAPERBACK ISBN: 979-8-3852-5885-7
HARDCOVER ISBN: 979-8-3852-5886-4
EBOOK ISBN: 979-8-3852-5887-1

VERSION NUMBER 090525

For

Joe, Tom, Katie

Beth, Tony, Marie

Charlie and Diane

The Stolen Child
Come away, Oh! human child
To The waters and the wild
With a faery, hand In hand,
For the world's more full of weeping
Then you can understand.

—W.B. Yeats

Contents

Acknowledgments

Grateful acknowledgment is made to my editor April Ossman and the editors of the journals and anthologies who first published the following poems. The poems, sometimes in earlier versions, appeared as follows:

The National League of American Pen Woman: "New Battles," "The Plague All Over Again," "The Gathering," "Once More With Feeling," "Eclipse Astro Philia", "In Memoriam."

Barnes Gallery: "Eclipse Astro Philia"

B.J. Spoke Gallery: "Manhattan," "The Gathering."

I

Eclipse Astro Philia

The greatest show I've seen on earth
maneuvered in the heavens
into a play of light haloing darkness,
a brief encounter of sun and moon
on a celestial stage,
casting its penumbra
onto the sun's photosphere,
as shadows sometimes reflect on my life.
I can almost hear the musical spheres,
echoing through the quiet world,
a celestial drama unfurling
before an audience whispering
a profound colloquy of awe,
rising to the rafters of God's cathedral
as mankind's prayer.

The Eagle Has Landed

We're not gathered in our comfortable home
to watch an impossibly distant Armstrong
alighting on the moon,
but rather in a buffeting wind
observing the mighty emblem of field and stream
perched atop the tallest evergreen.
A meteor among raptors,
the golden eagle locks his stare aimed from aloft
at today's unsuspecting prey below,
a dive so daring in its speed,
we gasped at his deadly grace,
a thunderbolt from above
piercing the lake with its talons,
amazing us with life's ancient paradox,
the taking of life to live.
Even vegans must kill to eat.

Awakening

Descending the High Sierra,
tracking in crackling snowmelt,
awakened by a bone-deep clock
that instinct alone can read,
slipping and sliding windward
to ice patches of uncertain dimensions,
she leads her two little bears,
nudging them on,
pursued by tracking wolves
hungry for a stray cub,
fording lakes and streams by day
to a valley of salmon and plenty,
devoted even when food is scarce,
awakening memories
of my mother's bear hugs.

The Gathering

Gather the children before the brassy world
transfigures their youthful radiance,
their innocence taken, as ours once was
betrayed by censorious controlling voices,
that silenced curiosity and wonder.

Gather alms from generous hands at church,
for the morning crowd of *Give us this day*,
making a feast from hunger,
in singing psalms of praise.

Gather the voices of migrants,
dimmed by consuming needs,
suffering in isolation,
welcome, feed and house them
as family with similar dreams.

Gather them all, domestic and foreign,
loved or forsaken, let the gentle tide
of our kindness lap
the shores of every land.

After living life on their knees,
may rising be their destiny.

Next Chapter

Before I leave our empty home,
one last embrace of memories,
family faces, fading to a time
remembered as a dream,
haunting these empty spaces.
In this bedroom, Beth's lace coverlet
tangled between her toes;
In Joe and Tom's, I give thanks
for some-time foes grown
to strongly bonded brothers.

My trinity of progeny,
Joe and Tom as hockey heroes,
Beth riding horses on the school field
as we cheered her on.
We laughed at Tom as Huck Finn,
and gasped at Joe in *Dial M For Murder*,
as he slinked across the school stage.
Beth charmed us as a lit Christmas tree.

We weathered together the sudden death
of Aunt Diane, and grandparents soon after,
and hopes denied when the varsity team
slipped beyond Tom's grasp,
and Daddy's business faltered.

I embrace every minute,
uncertain of my future memories' clarity,
or what new home could be as sweet.
Will my time be spent in a garden weeding,
planting forget-me-nots to seed a smile,
or wheelchair bound,
head drooping frail and needy,
with gentle ghosts as guides.

My Hour

Oh, I've strutted and fretted
my hour upon the stage,
I've played the part of Rosalind,
with childhood dreams recast,
a princess deprived of her inheritance,
but given a generous share
of sleepless nights and children's tears.

My imagined life's script,
revised by untimely deaths
of Diane and two good friends,
but salved by the epiphany
of grand-daughter, Katie.

Deep in the mind's caverns,
I embrace in their final stage,
dreams I can only imagine.

Once More With Feeling

When a comet from beyond,
the clouds sends starfish shooting
from the boiling ocean to the sky,
when the Earth gives up its matter,
and the blazing sun has died,
will the heavens be our lifeline,
another home to satisfy
our need to see it broken,
moon-scaped and unoccupied?
Will time on its cosmic flight

through space waste every planet
in its path, or engender
a quantum physics of possibility,
travelling in a transformed universe
to a new Eden beyond the abyss.

Hope

For every field a flowering meadow,
for every stream reclaimed from waste,
one living and breathing to take its place,
for every diaspora of wandering souls,
a harbor as the shore of home.

For every child a mother's love—
the rainbow of every storm,
the force that waves the water,
the face they greet dawn.

May lips that withhold kisses
and ears that refuse to hear,
overcome their pain and suffering
to face what they most fear.

Honora

More than a century ago,
five of her children
sailed to a foreign land
with dreams of every color,
leaving Honora
with young Patrick
tilling farmland that once
seemed heaven's green fields,
then wasted by famine and brutality,

I've come with family
to this land of Saints and Scholars,
placing flowers on Honora's grave,
a testament beyond our telling
of heartache, She gave it all,
and her spirit lives on in us.

The Darien Gap

Children limp on cut bare feet,
shoes sucked off by odorous mud,
their limbs weak and bruised.
Fearful and distraught,
mothers endure as always,
kissing and urging them on.
Fathers carry the youngest
on backs made strong by hard labor.
Swollen polluted streams
may drown them among venomous snakes,
disease or gang violence may erupt.
They trust because they must,
that a better place exists
beyond the Darien Gap.

The Doorway

All we missed of heaven on Earth,
we hope to find in your nation's plenty,
offering us haven from our native land
whose barbed wire and violence sent us.

Only your testimony of acceptance
is needed to feed ourselves,
for we are used to labor,
and bleeding goes unspoken.

Yes, we're tired and hungry,
the country we loved is dead,
our children are our promise,
as yours, in the years ahead,

Across a sea of uncertainty,
through many years of suffering,
to your open doorway, hopefuly,
in answer to freedom's call.

Your Valentine

Did your valentine get lost?
In truth I thought it would,
for I never licked the stamp
or sealed it as I should.

The sentiment was saccharine,
the words long overdue—
for remembering a time in our recent past,
cheap sentiment lost in transit will do.

If this sounds a bit unfair;
maybe the truth should be shared;
our lovemaking amounted to a Lenten fast.

Something beyond weak explanation,
maybe another life?
Maybe a strong temptation
frayed your moral fiber.

A thumbnail of the game you played
will tell my story—
She held a hand full of aces
while he had all the spades.

Ordinary Beauty

A gusty wind buffets a red-tailed hawk,
and still he climbs,
as far below a coyote creeps
closer to cooing pigeons,
while the scarlet tanager
fresh from the foothills,
builds her shallow nest in the treetops.
Awakening wildflowers will recover
from the fawn nibling their foliage.
The rising sun brightens the leaves
and disperses the drifting mist,
all inhaled and tasted, transforming
our mountains of complaints
to a grassy hill, where we spread a picnic,
amid nature's gifts.

The Heron

Quietly, I stalk the heron's path
through the tufted reeds,
trying not to splash
as I wade into his bath.
His mesmerizing pose,
white as bone, still as stone,
drew me to this muddy pond,
where I caused his fearful flight.
If only I could tell him how
and why, my words can't say
how much I lament his leaving.

In Memoriam

The sound of silence is remade
by the voice of the wilderness,
where hawks breach
the high Sierras ghostly mists.
The Giant Sequoia,
the largest living thing on earth,
felled in such numbers
as to fell comprehension,
a tremendous cascade
of environmental destruction
tumbling into the Kaweah river.

Wild wings seeking shade
flee from the barren landscape,
the west winds upward draft echo
an ode to the haunted abyss,
a majestic forest even God will miss.

Coming Soon to a Tree Near You

In the wind and the woods,
light as a leaf tangled
in twigs and twine,
harvested for avian nests
by mates of a feather
for their noisy crew,
spurning the new birdhouse
painted in robin's-egg blue,
instead building a nest
under my blueberry bush,
brooding new songbirds
to hop on my lawn
in search of early worms.
A friendly family of warblers
to serenade me with morning song
and warm red breasts.

The Rose and the Dandelion

I wandered lovely as a rose vine
unique among the petaled,
until dandelions piqued my pride
when their blooms outpaced mine.

Prolific as its seeds can be,
the go-to weed given freely,
feeds the goldfinch all summer
and makes cheap wine for fall.

The blooming curse of every lawn,
my friend says rides every storm,
bestowing unwelcome seeds
too multitudinous to defeat.

The Diner Party

I accepted the invitation
to rebalance my lonely life,
when host Ted welcomed
my moving in next door.
He seeks me out with an encouraging nod,
and proffers a glass of chardonnay.
Just as a pontificating politician is cautioned
that his opinions are toxic,
a zoftig matron in a red dress
undermines her superior expression
by tugging at her hanging bra strap,
as she joins the misbehaving guests,
accompanied by sophisticated strings,
singing off-key and increasingly tipsy,
a virtual tinder box of possibilities,
I anticipate another fourth of July.
Foibles are charming when you're lonesome.
With the guests all seated,
we start our conversation tentatively.
I smile and nod, freeze when I disagree,
disarming any potential adversaries,
a sensible plan in this age of anxiety,
long past the age of innocence.
No Judas to my host am I—
hopeful of repeat communions.

II

For Priests

Follow the man who kissed the leper,
and believe you will stay free;
with a wolf at his side, he lived
like a lamb wandering Muslim lands.

Follow the man who heard confessions
of sin and despair each day,
offering the love of divine repair,
instead of the seat of judgment.

Follow the man who walked on water,
he will never let you drown;
his arms lift you up, undeserving,
to share his divine fellowship.

Follow his footprints in the sand,
and know when they're washed away,
your image remains just the same,
in the person his shadow became.

Abide With Me

My astral self alone at dawn
as night stars faded into day,
I saw luminous forms
long departed from this life,
some of whom in my childhood
caused wounds that still haunt me,
What a long memory you have, they said.
Why carry all that around?
But where can I put it down, I asked.
Whereas with others who loved me
from first sight, I see beyond
the dust carried by stellar winds
to the outermost universe,
joining a family reunion never imagined,
whose mother tongue requires
the forgiveness we all desire.

Twilight for Maryann

Old friends in faith,
as young nursing students
walking to the chapel
next door to the morgue.

Years past our better days,
we embrace, frail, but purposeful
beyond all need of explaining,
our lives made bare
by the loss of friends we loved,
comforted yes, by grandchildren,
who nevertheless don't comprehend
the test of lost vigor,
and dreams endlessly deferred.

Will this be our epilogue,
written with my fleeting talent,
and your fading memory,
inspired by Milton's words
as he met his fate, *They also serve*
who only stand and wait.

St. Joseph's Choir

Sopranos fly almost to heaven,
altos aim for the rafters,
as tenors manly notes surpass
even Joe and Jerry's sounds.
The flute in drifting melody
played by Mark in *Celtic Laud*,
as lyrical as Irish poetry,
Amazing Grace and Glory Be
choir swelling, chorus bending
the soul of *Song of the Sea*.
Marie directs with inspired hands
as angels join in felicity,
their voices blending
in our heavenly choir
of just pretending.

The Plague All Over Again

Smart phones and the internet
can't dry the world's tears
or baptize the dying elderly
and vibrantly young.
Passionate men and women
who thought they would die
in their own good time,
can't even whisper
through their ventilators.
The bereaved pray and prepare,
as in every plague in history,
hoping spiritus takes wing
as another breathless life begins
the dawning days of the dead.

Abba

The day fell
like the Cedars of Lebanon,
splintering my consciousness,
though when I opened
the door, the quiet came
from his room like a friend
whispering words of comfort,
the breathless sound
of his loving life, leaving me
alone, trying to remember
when last he held me fast,
his melodious voice and artful talent
now performing transformed,
returning to the source
from which it came—
but *Oh!* How I'll miss him,
just the same.

Frankie, I Miss You

Try as I may to express it,
Frankie said it best,
he barked on call,
rocking and rolling
at the doorbell's tone,
testing my eardrums
with his decibels.

Did I know how much he loved me,
when he followed me around?
Did he think I could guess
the wisdom in his loud
and faithful sounds?

I miss him as I sip my coffee,
but later miss him more,
when his friends come sniffing
at the gate, their sad stares
that seems to say—
Have we come too late?

Forgiveness

Forgiveness doesn't alter the wound,
but bears it as an echo,
ethereal sounding, but earthly bound
to its source, as muscle to myoma,
as inspiration is to poetry moving us
to human understanding,
seeing ourselves in a mirror,
bound to *the fragrance the violet sheds,*
clinging fast to the heel that crushed it,
blow by blow, but maybe better said,
as the laurel and the ivy know.

Gone for Now

Before the avalanche
of stormy days weathering my life,
to the evening you died
in the sundown of our lives,
stealing away what was sanctified,
to the valley of prayers denied,

but I hear you say
from beyond the grave
that you still see my loving face,
and the forget-me-nots
I planted in remembrance
rebloom in your embrace.

Grandparents

They disappeared one day,
before I knew them as individuals.
My Nana made our clothes
and baked fresh bread for us.
Papa drew nudes,
but not I think at work,
as sextant at our church.
They never used technology,
and seemed smaller as I grew.
Intent on leaving childhood
behind to experience life,
never again knowing such kindness,
until my partner's betrayal sent me
back to those watchful protectors
death has since taken away.
They grow taller in memory,
I can almost hear them say
how much they still love me,
in their sweet Gaelic way.

Time Passed

Have I passed the joy of life,
as when I climbed Croagh Patrick,
and breathed the saintly air,
or when I saw a young man
at the beach in his glory?
Perhaps I can still feel passion
untested these many years,
waiting for the right palpitations,
but other loves call in memories
of my childhood home,
an aroma of gentleness
my wandering mind returns to,
searching, my lifelong quest
for a heaven of the heart
to fill my emptiness.

Would You Do It Over Again?

Would you listen again
to your mother repeating
words you heard as a child.
She saw the world
with more innocent eyes,
while you felt your temperature rising.

Would you make Communion again
in a homemade lace dress,
and commit to Jesus,
until life interfered,
and *always* became leap years.

Would you let Ted kiss you
good-by again, knowing
and not asking why,
he reluctantly attended your wedding,
then abandoned his priesthood,
and the church he loved.

Would you give up your sins,
even those that feel like wins;

Would you do it all over again?

Leonard

My mother died, he solemnly said,
I must go home today,
his words falling like snow,
bare as the cold air.
Is it true I wondered,
would he lie about such things?
Leonard knows me well enough
to wait here Sunday mornings,
when I have to pass him by,
opening my book of church music
with my wallet tucked inside.
I hope small bills will be enough:
How much is the ride?

This Love

It never was meant to be carved in stone,
but to lift us like feathers on the wind,
with beauty born of a variety
that the world well knows,
attuned to other's needs,
rising to the height
of unmeasured distance
across a sublime eternity,
to the vestibule of paradise
backward in time,
before the world was made
to be embraced anew by a love
that only yesterday
kissed my upturned face.

Forgiveness Aubade

Falling as poetry on the frozen ground,
snow keeps my words warm,
this cloudy night dimming every star.
Rising into tomorrow, the blazing sun
diffuses beauty in rays of hazy light,
casting my long shadow in the melting snow
as I leave to pick up my estranged brother,
coming home at last for his mea culpa.

Mindful of memories,
hoping maturity may give us pause,
his gentle words
and morning birdsong share
a promise of forgiveness in aubade,
alighting on branches of old oak,
echoing sounds of truth to power
to serve me well this difficult dawn,
where our rising sun belongs.

Mother Most Loved

Her hands kneaded bread so well,
her words blessed us as we ate it,
the wealth of her Gaelic songs,
shared as Irish families do;
she played a mean piano
while we sang off-key.
Before I left for college she gave me

a homemade suit of Botany tweed,
a full measure of her pride in me,
and a dream.

My mother of many talents,
baking, sewing, singing, planting,
I sit in the garden whispering her name,
and from the fragrance of the foliage—
Olive, please come home,
your roses are fearful of dying alone.

Far and Away

I arrived at the Newfoundland ruins
of my mother's Salmonier home,
with warm sun on my face,
and salty winds tangling my hair.
I walked among the hills she knew,
the bees incessant buzzing among
wild goldenrod and pitcher plants,
the green grass being eaten
by billy goats like the ones
who once butted Mom into the mud.
I hear her voice as I hum her *Celtic Laud:*
For the dove in the sky,
For the wind in the trees.
Like my mother, I am a wanderer.
She missed her home and family,
but not the controlling influence
of the church on her neighbors,
and the poverty
that couldn't be denied.

I watched over the sea-walled coast,
as the twisting, raging foam
sprayed salt water on our faces.
I stood at rocky outcrops
where fierce Atlantic storms
have hurled boats and fishermen
to their deaths, and give thanks
to her old home for gifting
my mother to me.

De Profundis

Thank you for coming, and color me excited
to be where everyone knows my name.
Some of you I haven't seen in years,
none I'd want to miss this momentous occasion.
When I drove by my house on the way home,
mallards flocked to their morning meal,
the newspaper on the doormat heralded my absence,
the forget-me-nots bloomed as they always have,
everything is as it was—
except my being taken where I don't want to go,
in a fitting transport for my second coming.

As my requiem begins, and voices hymn,
As the saints come marching in,
I remember the last time
I was escorted down the aisle,
everyone smiling, Charlie at the altar.
I wonder where he waits now,
as I join the litany of luminous souls,
occasioned by God's command,
Lay down your life, Come as you are,
an invitation I couldn't refuse,
as I move past the grave's absolution,
to dive wholly into whatever mystery
the depths of heaven protect.
Pray that I arrive safely,
in *that undiscovered country,*
from which no one has ever returned.

III

Manhattan

It's a place of mansions and flophouses,
where poverty and plenty co-exist.
One man on the street has holes in his clothes,
another is meeting Mayor Adams.

I sip coffee on an early train,
to see Shakespeare's *Macbeth*,
with time to visit St. Patrick's
and smell the saintly air.

In Bryant Park, begging hands
in the sundown of their lives
still share their crumbs with pigeons.

One day if justice drifts their way,
In the ebb and flow of tides,
A safe harbor will be found,
And for their lives a new beginning
with a better ending,
though they may never meet the mayor,
or take the train to see Macbeth.

City Lights

Republican or Democrat,
I think you would agree
that red or blue, they all pursue
only marginal degrees of honesty.

With politicians at the helm,
winds of opportunity abound,
the deals that benefit them all
remain hidden at City Hall.

With talk of cutting crime,
pick-pockets should beware:
stop-and-frisk are the go-to
for the law-and-order crowd,

As rats run free and multiply
on streets and in Central Park,
heading south for bread line,
with nary a pied piper in sight.

Surprise!

I sincerely desired upon expiring,
a place of heavenly wisdom,
reserved for the few
who gave the best view
of love whatever the season.

Well, What a surprise
to see the sun rise
on a cookout with God's favorite people,
the poor man, who begged at the train,
the sinners, who were never to blame,
the insane and saints unaware
of why they are even there.

I like them all myself,
but I have my favorites—
especially those never to blame,
and some of my friends
you may call insane.
God knows what's best,

but lacking in wealth or ambition,
my making friends depending
on innocent ends,
goes well beyond intuition.

I'm glad to tend the fire
at this cook-out for all,
everyone innocently greeting
the neighbor in the stranger's face,
at a picnic of heavenly wisdom.

To Katie, After the Graduation Party

Are you thinking of saving the money
I saw you stash in your socks
hidden under the bed?
Why not spend those greenbacks
on photo-friendly events,
and post them to go viral,
making you a fortune
for your influence.

Over the top advice you think?
What I'm trying to say Katie,
is *Life's a cabaret,*
though your daddy won't agree.
Why sit alone in your room,
when the world is waiting—
go play your tune.

You're on your own, don't need me
for your symphony,
but I hope you ask me to visit.

Enough of Time

I only know Him in my running
on my hometown favorite trail,
as the leaves' windy symphony
soothes my aching limbs.

I only know Him in my singing
from the choir loft above,
altos ascending to the rafters
notes sweet as peaches on my tongue.

I only know Him in my weeping
over malignant tumors multiplied,
claustrophobic scans, dissection,
terrified prayers and curettage.

I only know Him in my playing
in a sandbox built for two,
Katie's little voice requesting
loving hands to raise her castle.

I only know Him in my hoping,
when all my seasons have passed,
quotidian moments of faith, embraced
as inspiration, won't be my last.

The Cloud of Unknowing

I saw the number seven on a road sign,
a number that means you're ready
for your spiritual path to open.
It seemed so perfect and complete
in its upright leaning, that I drove until
darkness clouded mind and body,
with the ghosts of lost loves
whose names I've misplaced.
Shall I linger here courageous,
or move beyond night-watching stars,
into the cloud of unknowing,
abandoning my mind and ego
to that realm of uncertainty without image,
where human consciousness surrenders,
embracing that divine source
of inward and outward enlightenment.

Musings

I may swear by all that's holy,
then again by all that's true—
no matter how self-defensive,
the force that moves mountains
makes me often think of you.

Then again by all I hoped for
in my life of loves and loss,
not Shakespearean immortality,
but a spot in the divine mind,
even as an afterthought.

May my alchemy of matter, prayer and poetry,
that in His likeness was sometimes seen,
as when I saw beyond my suffering,
soon be changed into his image,
or maybe something in between.

One day my life of words and keyboards
in my dreams may raise me high,
beyond the praise of my muse,
bragging to the angels:
        She is very well-read.

Nature's Transformation

When even insistent violets cease to bloom,
and the sweet-smelling earth
reeks of toxins from destroyed cities,
when hurricanes, wildfires, floods,
and droughts rage, devastating fields and waterways,
where species once roamed wild and free,
before we brought them to their knees.

When the Statue of Liberty drowns in rising seas,
ruined as the statue of Ozymandias
exposed above the hot hungry sand,
will anyone be left to lament
what we did to our planet,
to the naked, bleak and baking land,
with hubris as great as that ancient
king of kings?

Silence

As silent snowflakes blanket
the burrows of voles and mice,
the sun dawns on Ukraine's
former breadbasket
turned scarred battlefield,
the land, soldiers and children
blasted equally by bombs.

Come away, Russia, leave your weapons,
form your battalions
with your astral remnant,
from this earthwork of war and open graves
with an invocation to return your life force
embarking on a new initiative:
the green fields of peace.

New Battles

Now Gaza burns at the stake,
soon to be remaking
a famine field of abundant yields,

where mothers and children
once played in the park,
before drones and bombs
silenced their joy
and flung their severed limbs.

Dawning upon the mourning landscape,
on the shores of nevermore,
like Milton's blindness,
the rising sun seems unaware
the fallen world's no longer there.

Ukraine Then and Now

They fought then for independence,
when all the world was at war,
and freedom was so dearly bought
that innocence lost its human face.

Today, we rally the soldiers on,
as they fight and die to hold the line,
in trenches wet with human blood,
to defend their sovereign nation
against buzzing drones foretelling
wounded and fallen men.

Bearing each other's sufferings,
raised by their comrades to a state of grace,
tearful in the enveloping smoke shroud,
seeming to evoke heaven's pity
on the embodied wasteland

Afghanistan

For many years, hand in hand,
driven the way of desperate souls
fearful and cold in the winter air,
families escaped the hostile land,
but hunger took its toll.

A culture ancient as the Khyber Pass,
enduring invasions of conquerors,
but Taliban rule brought extreme justice
with bleeding stumps of thieves'
and the terror of severed heads,
in a land bereaved.

A war-torn country of men, women,
and hungry orphans, their faces wasted,
enduring a life betrayed,
by baskets of rotting harvests,
the starving lay down exhausted
in the drifting dust,
Waiting for hope to transfigure
the wasteland.

Darfur, Sudan

The house is empty, the table blood-stained,
still holding broken crockery.
Forced to see their mother's rape,
the children were made to move on,
starved and scorned.

The war of settled farmers needing water
fighting nomadic herdsmen needing land,
is turning hands meant for plowing
to wage sex abuse and death.

Are we not Human,
in our suffering?,
they ask as in years past,
hoping again for aid
from hands that gave before.

Out of Africa once came Eden.
Out of suffering came Darfur.

A Tribute to Challenger and Titan for July 4th

Into the delirious burning blue
and darkest depths of the ocean,
Challenger's crew forged their epitaphs,
a bold thrust into a new age
to seize the day for mankind,
knocking at destiny's door.

Titan's heroes sank beneath the sea,
imploding their ghosts,
a requiem in the North Atlantic,
their last full measure igniting lamps
for those who come after.

Old Glory

Waving in the unfurled air,
saluted by men foresworn to freedom,
or in a proud window
for a gold star mother's grief.
It marches in loud parades
of homemade happiness.
It blew from Old Ironsides' mast,
and draped the 9–11 firefighters,
joining a long blue line to heaven,
flying over homes, churches too,
then half-staff with drums and fife,
over tombs unknown, it flies for life,
enduring all that we and the wind demand.

Remember Us

We came here in our salad days,
when we were green,
rosy as tomatoes before life
grayed our hair, lined our faces,
and death took what was due.
We were so foolish then
as to laugh at dismay,
though I won't say we wasted time,
being mindful enough to savor it.

I return today,
to the Americana Hotel,
alone at the table that remembers us,
our clams still on the half shell.
Just a drink will do—
and for my friends a few,
to toast what once was ours:

Charlie and Audrey,
bellying up to the bar,
the best of years by far.

My First Psalm

The dearest, freshness, deep down things
are universal seeds germinating fields of wheat,
as God's grace engendered mine,
the most unlikely of womankind,
who saw herself as nature's gift,
lacking a spiritual fit,
where a beaten path was hard to find.
I became the sediment
of a benevolent shore,
with poets' praise and social change
the ramparts of my new shalom,
where fallen angels, appropriately
sent by God to rescue me,
illuminated the shadowlands of life
that had held me fast,
in the embrace of my own will,
with new visions of brotherhood.

The Wild Ones

No puma came down from the hills
to hunt buffalo on the prairie,
but the grass remembers both.
The bison diminished, but still powerful
in the echoes of thundering hooves,
his little friend the prairie dog,
aerates the wild golden grass
bending in the wind.
Missing from the hunt—
the Comanche who buried their dreams
along the trail of tears,
their sun-dancing ghosts haunt the plains
with the thunder of galloping horses,
echoing those of the buffalo
wild in spirit, gone from a vanished land.

Notes

"My First Psalm" quotes a line from G.M.Hopkins, "God's Grandeur."

"Afghanistan" quotes a line from T.S. Eliot, "The Wasteland."

"A Tribute to Challenger and Titan" quotes a line from John Magee, "High Flight."

"Twilight for Maryann" quotes a line from John Milton, "On His Blindness."

www.ingramcontent.com/pod-product-compliance
Lightning Source LLC
LaVergne TN
LVHW020658100826
845148LV00012B/2554

* 9 7 9 8 3 8 5 2 5 8 8 5 7 *